101 Ways to ~~Heat~~ Survive a Broken Heart

By Kevin Adcraft

101 WAYS TO ~~HEAL~~ SURVIVE A BROKEN HEART

By Kevin R. Adcroft

Illustrations by Benjamin Adcroft

ACKNOWLEDGEMENT

Thank you God. To my family who gave me hope when I was at the end of my rope! To my sons who always inspire me to be the best person I can be. Benjamin without your creativity and artistic talent this book would not exist, you added a hundred and one thousand words worth of pictures. Jordan, you patiently matched the pictures to the words from hundreds of illustrations, and are always there to help make my crazy ideas into crazier realities. To my Mom whose faith and love are unparalleled. Noel thanks for the kindness, generosity and candy and Pat for your hospitality and real food. To my brother Sean whose wit and humor always put a smile on my face and who came up with the idea to make this an illustrated book.

I'm appreciative to all of my aunts, uncles, nieces and nephews and all of my cousins for their strength, faith and love. To my brother Joe and his wife Margie who let me hold up in your home after I smashed my car (repeatedly). To my brother Bobby who always has a positive attitude and his wife Bernie who always welcomes me with a plate of food and some tea. Marilu and Toby thanks for opening your home and making my California dreaming come true. Norine and Bob thanks for your love and support.

Dooley I never would have gotten this book done without the patience it must have taken to work with me and my second grade reading and writing level. It was more like transcribing hieroglyphics than anyone will ever know. To my sister in law Martina the marathoner.

My Sister Patti, whose strength and courage were a great example. To my Dad, whose hard work ethic was instilled in all of us at a very young age.

Tommy Burns, you're like a brother to me. Jonathan Stewart, I still have the surf board!

Tommy Siddons who sold me the VW Bus for 200 bucks, that Bus saved my life Bro.

Tony Robbins who inspired me and Adam Sandler who made me laugh even in the darkest of nights. To Bishop Dougherty, who mysteriously showed up at my door one night, when I wanted to end my life. I'm very grateful to Mary Theresa Patterson whose wise council went well beyond legal help.

To the awesome power of love in the world that's always there in each of us just waiting to be tapped into and set free. To the part of each of our souls that connects us to one another and all of us to the universe.

To everyone reading this book, your broken heart will heal in time, and although we have never met, I thank you and love you for being you. Your love is a testament to the love and kindness in the world! All that love in your heart is just what the world needs to make it a better place, so please don't quit. Some day maybe we will meet and then you will see that I am you and you are me, and love is the answer!

If you've picked up this book, I urge you not to put it down. I don't care if you read it in the bookstore or go to the library and read it. Borrow it. Beg for it. Do whatever you have to. It could save your life. I wouldn't wish the feeling of a broken heart on my worst enemy. I know where you are coming from. You're carrying this pain and despair. You've got to hang on. Hang on, help is on the way. I've lived through this hell and you can survive it too.

I had self-destructive thoughts and contemplated suicide. I got as far as climbing up into the barn in my backyard, putting a rope around my neck and experiencing the feeling of having it tied there. If you are at the end of your rope and you can no longer deal with it, please read this book. Just follow what I say, follow what I did and you'll make it through. One minute at a time. Just keep breathing. I've been where you are. I know the pain. You can make it through another day, even when it feels like you can't go another moment. Help is on the way. Help is right here.

At the end of my marriage my brother-in-law borrowed a rifle that belonged to me. I told him that I wanted it back. Well he returned the rifle to me, but everyone was very concerned that I would either kill myself or go on a rampage and kill my wife, which I had no intention of doing.

I just wanted my rifle back, but because of everyone's paranoia I said that I would get rid of it. I sold it. I actually sold it to my father-in-law. I said "Here, I'll sell you the rifle. I'm not going to do anything with it."

In hindsight, I realize that it was a good idea to get rid of the rifle, because there were times that when I got into those deep, deep thoughts of despair and depression. All logic and reason went out the window. Sometimes you find yourself in such a rut, that you feel like you're not going to get out and it looks pretty comforting looking at the barrel of the rifle. So if you have something like that get rid of it. So if you have firearms, it might be a good idea to give them to someone else to hold on to. Or just sell them and be rid of them.

Now you are going through an incredibly difficult time in your life, so you are entitled to feel sorry for yourself sometimes. Don't be under the illusion that you'll feel better by lying in bed just curled up in the fetal position afraid to move. If you find yourself curled up in the fetal position in bed or on a couch for hours or days on end, feeling sorry for yourself, feeling deep depression or despair, visualize one thing. YOU ARE NOT LYING ON A COUCH. YOU ARE NOT LYING IN BED. YOU ARE IN THE MIDDLE OF THE OCEAN SURROUNDED BY SHARKS! Those sharks are going to kill you if you don't get the f#*k out of there. Get the f*#k out of the water. Start swimming for shore.

Get out. Swim for shore. Move! Get out of that damn bed right now. Start walking. Start running. Start moving. Move your body. Move immediately. Start moving. If you have to run out of your house, even if you don't have on socks or shoes, start running, don't stop running, keep moving. You must move your body. Staying there, you'll die.

Visualize that you just touched a live wire. If you found yourself being electrocuted you have to ask someone, or hope that someone saw you and hit you with a big piece of wood, or a board or 2X4 to move you away from the wire frying you. You've got to get free from that electrical juice.

Again, at all costs you've got to move. If it means picking up the phone and calling somebody, do it. If you cannot physically run, dial the number, call somebody, do not stay where you are, or you will die. Move. Do whatever it takes, just move.

When you're in love with someone, you tend to think that person is perfect. I suffered from this delusion. I really and truly felt my ex was perfect. That is an unfair expectation to have. No one is perfect.

I needed to make a clean break. I know you may be saying we have kids together, a house, maybe even a business. Well if this kills you, then what the hell good are you to your kids. If you are anything like me, then this is a matter of life and death, namely YOURS!

I can't tell you the number of people I have known over the years that have literally killed themselves over a broken heart. I am not one of them, although I thought about it. Here is my story.

If I made it, then you can too. We had two boys, Benjamin and Jordan. We had multiple houses. Yes we had a business together. Even with these complications, it was critical that I cut off all contact. And here is how to do it. You must block all feelings for that person. Yes I said block them. Screw the therapist if he's telling you to feel them. In your mind, your ex is dead. The person you're dealing with (your EX) is just a shitty overpaid baby sitter you have to have. The way I see it, you have two choices. One, you tell yourself your wife or husband (or significant other) was killed in an automobile accident or two they didn't love you because you are a worthless piece of shit. I don't know about you, but I am not a piece of shit.

Unfortunately, you will need to hire a lawyer if you had kids or real estate and/or a business together. If it would not kill you to be around your EX you would likely not be reading this book and you might be able to come up with an amicable agreement without involving lawyers. That was not the case for me.

Through the grace of God I got a great lawyer who helped save my life. She quickly realized that I might not make it and suggested that I get help. Yes I went to a therapist. Yes I took medication. Pills to calm down. Pills for depression. Pills to sleep. Yes they told me to feel the feelings. That was a big problem. If I could not stop feeling it was going to kill me. I had to block it out, if only for a little while. When I told myself that my wife was killed in an automobile accident I felt better.

What was killing me? It was that she did not love me. I know it may sound twisted, but I needed to think this way to survive. I was going weeks and weeks with very little to no sleep. Even with sleeping pills.

The more I blocked out the reality of her not loving me, the better I felt. I told myself that my wife was tragically killed in an auto accident. I still missed her and was heartbroken that she was dead, but somehow I summoned the will to go on. I guess because I did not feel like a worthless piece of shit. My life still mattered. When I picked up my boys from the "shitty baby sitter" I told myself that this person had a disease and if her hand touched mine or I got too close I would catch it.

As far as the business and houses went, I let the lawyers handle that. Almost everything was lost. That really didn't bother me. You see my boys were still alive. They were not killed in the car accident. Material things really had no value to me.

Even if you do not have kids, or own real estate or have a business together it is important for you to cut off all contact. You need time to heal. Don't pick at the scab. You will open up the wound and start bleeding. Stay away from his or her house. Don't even think about checking Facebook or anything like that.

If they try calling you or emailing you tell them that they ended it and you need time away. Maybe someday you can talk and be friends but not now. If they don't get the message when you are nice, you may have to tell them to leave you the F#*K alone.

If you have to block their calls, do it. On the other hand if you are calling them and emailing, etc., then STOP NOW. You are prolonging the pain. You need to be like a race horse. Put the blinders on and focus on other things.

DISCLAIMER

The 101 suggestions for surviving a broken heart that follow are based on the actual experiences of Kevin R. Adcroft. They are, in essence, his story. He honestly believes that they helped him survive the most difficult period in his life. Mr. Adcroft is not a psychiatrist, psychologist, therapist or mental health professional, nor does he play one on TV. Please check your state and local laws and ordinances if you have any questions about the legality of the advice herein. Your mileage may vary, yours will probably be less. The number for the National Suicide Prevention Hotline is: 1-800-273-8355.

1. **CRY** – to call out; shout; weep; to proclaim publicly; to advertise wares by calling out: a loud outcry, appeal, entreaty: a fit of weeping the characteristic sound uttered by an animal.

This is the definition in Webster's Dictionary and if you are able to, do it. This will help. If not, I know how you feel. You might wish you could but nothing happens. It feels like you just got run over by a tractor trailer. The pain is unbearable. You can't eat, can't sleep, you can't stop thinking about her or him. Your mind keeps racing. You think if only you had done this or that, then maybe they would not have broken up with me. You are really whipping yourself into a real frenzy. You are becoming overwhelmed by it. Pain, despair, depression. I became very close to those three. I wrote a song about it.

Pain, despair, depression are my lovers
They fuck with me every day!
Despair she sleeps with me every night.
Suicide, sweet suicide how you long to hold me in your arms
And never let me go!

Hang on. If I survived it, so can you!

2

2.	**BREATHE** - inhale for five seconds and hold for twenty. Exhale for ten seconds. If you can keep breathing you will make it through. Focus on your breath, inhale threw the nose for five seconds. Feel the air filling you up. Take a deep diaphragmatic breath, hold for 20 seconds, then, exhale for ten seconds. The ratio is inhale one count, hold four counts, exhale two counts So if you would like you can change it to seven second inhale, twenty-eight second hold, fourteen second exhale. That's okay, whatever works for you. Do ten sets of these anytime you are feeling overwhelmed. Also get into the habit of doing them in the morning, mid day and at night. These exercises done consistently three times a day will help tremendously. Remember I am an expert at surviving a broken heart and I did this and it works. If you want to feel better do this for the next thirty days and see what happens. You may find that you feel so much better that you will keep doing it. In all kinds of yoga meditation they talk about how important your breathing is. Without it you would be dead. So just keep on breathing.

3. **LIE DOWN AND FEEL SORRY FOR YOURSELF** - this is a sad sick feeling that will make you want to move a heavy weight on your chest. Like a dog who just got run over by a truck. You will be afraid to move because the pain might get worse. You will feel despair and a lot of self pity. The good news is that you will eventually hit rock bottom. At this time the pain will level off. You will become numb. Like a zombie. When you reach this point you feel like you are in a bad dream. Although this feeling will last a while it does not get any worse. It's like being punch drunk. You will become used to it. The empty, sick, lonely feeling. Take comfort in knowing that you have nowhere to go but up. You will feel better in the future.

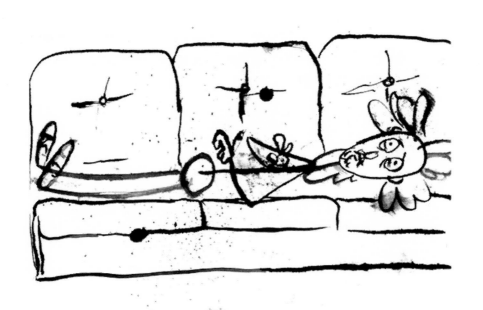

4.   **GET DRUNK** – At first you will think it's helping you feel better. Then all of a sudden it will hit you. You will go through all stages. Denial, anger, sadness. This is what helped me cry. I just kept drinking to dull the pain, if only for a few minutes. Well I kept drinking and drinking, then I got angry. I started yelling at my brother telling him his life was perfect. What the hell did he know about pain. Then denial. Thinking maybe she will call me and tell me she was sorry and wanted to get back together.

When sadness came it hit like a tidal wave. I then could not stop crying. What a difference, I was crying like a baby. I can't remember being more pathetic than I was at this time in my life. Finally I guess I passed out. The next day when I woke up I was as sick as a dog. I thought being run over by a tractor trailer was bad, well now I was throwing up and could not even walk. I was crawling to get from one room to the next. Finally I just stayed in the bathroom. On second thought maybe you should skip the getting drunk!

5.   **PRAY** - There is a term called foxhole prayer. I think it came from when men found themselves sitting in a fox hole and bombs were going off around them. They suddenly found religion or God. Well I am not suggesting you should just turn to God or prayer because you are having a tough time. I think when people are going through life they have a time when you realize that there is a higher power, which I call God. This is a time you can get close to your higher power. Opening your heart and soul to find your conscience. If you want to find the strength to make it through another day this is the answer. God don't make junk and he created you for a purpose. Somewhere deep inside your heart and soul you will begin to feel that you are part of the universe; at the core of your being is pure LOVE. This is what I believe we are. If you love sincerely, health, passion and growth will come. Start at the core of your being and let it all come out of you, that which you give you will receive.

6.   **QUIT DRINKING** - If you are feeling sad or depressed it will help you feel better if you quit drinking after all. Alcohol is a depressant. Not only that, but it kills brain cells and if you are anything like me you can't afford to kill any of those. Now if you have trouble quitting we might have opened up a can of worms. In this case get help! Go to AA meetings. Do 90 meetings in 90 days. Get a sponsor and work the twelve steps. This program saves lives. There are some meetings that are called open meetings, this is a meeting that anyone could go to. You don't have to feel as though you have to talk, just listen and learn. There are many 12 step programs and they will all help. Coda, Al-anon, etc. If you're having trouble, get the help you need. If you are able to quit and have no trouble, then good for you. Try to find the positives in quitting: saving money, saving brain cells, saving your life. That's a lot of savings. You are building a nice nest egg.

7. **GO FOR A WALK/RUN** – Walking will help you feel better. There are all kinds of positive effects from walking. First and foremost, it is good for your health. If you are not in good physical condition start slow and check with your doctor before you over do it. It will help calm your mind. You can save money on gasoline if you walk to the bank, post office or other errands you need to do. You start to notice things you have been missing. Maybe there are some trees you walk by that you never noticed. Or an old house or building that has some interesting architecture. You may hear birds sing, or someone playing guitar or piano. Ever play loud music, but as you walk you notice that things are changing from block to block. What a variety! Or maybe not, maybe you are walking along the beach or field and things are the same each quarter mile. Then enjoy the peacefulness of your view. You may even feel like running. Go ahead try. Remember when you were a kid running and playing outside? You know something that kid is still inside of you. Let him or her out and you will have fun.

8.   **SCREAM** – Every once in a while let out a big scream. When you are driving in your car scream. Put the windows up and let out a big scream. Pretend you are in an acting class and they are looking for someone to star in the next big horror film. They walk up to you and say: "Let's hear you scream." Then they say: "That's all you've got." Of course you can do better than that. Well now they said they are remaking an old Alfred Hitchcock movie, Psycho and you have to practice in the shower. So when you get home and are taking a shower remember to practice making the perfect scream. Well you did not get the part but there is a George of the Jungle show and if you can scream like George you can have that part. So the next time you step outside your door, just scream.

9. **TURN ON THE TV** – If you are looking for a distraction turn on your TV. I love watching infomercials. They make me feel like there is a chance I could make it. I sent away for money making deals. My favorite is in real estate no money down. I have gotten Russ Whitney, which is my favorite, Carlton Sheets, Tom Woo, Ed Beckley and probably a few others I can't even remember. I remember sending for the Credit Card Millionaire System, this really worked for me I am able to do it (not that I became a millionaire). I am really entertained by infomercials. Someday I would like to have my own. Plus the TV goes on 24/7 so it is always there for you, to keep you company. I could just keep watching and watching and watching. One show follows the next. It is like another world. It's like a drug that's always available and it's not even illegal. You can take as much as you want and you will not go to jail.

10. **Go see a Therapist** – Be careful about the therapist you select. Maybe you have a family member or friend who could recommend someone for you. I just picked one randomly out of the phone book and they suggested taking pills with the side effect of breast enlargement and loss of hair. This therapist truly felt that I was suicidal and I was afraid that she was going to call 911 and have the men in the white suits with strait jackets pick me up. She finally agreed to let me leave her office if I called and had a family member pick me up. I think because I had not slept in about four days. Some of what I was saying concerned her. Still I think it did me good to talk to someone. I also did start taking the anti-depressants she suggested. In hind sight I don't know if the pills were a good idea. I'm really not happy about having big tits and being bald. Some anti-depressants have the side effect of causing suicidal thoughts. So please be careful. The pill thing, well you'll have to decide it for yourself.

11. **Go visit** - your sister or brother or cousin or friend or someone. Just go visit a person. See how they are doing. How is life going for someone else. Maybe they need help fixing something in their apartment or house. They might want to move some furniture around, my sister did and she appreciated the help. As I was helping her move stuff I saw an old guitar. I picked it up and hit a few strings then I asked her if I could borrow it to play with. She said sure. She got it years ago and had started to learn, then just stopped playing it. If your sister or brother or cousin or friend or a person you are visiting does not have a guitar, keep visiting until you find someone who does have one. Don't stop until you find a guitar. If a long time has gone by and still no guitar, then go to the Salvation Army or a second hand shop or look in Paper Shop. If still no luck just go out and buy a guitar!

12. **TAKE GUITAR LESSONS** - from three different teachers at the same time. Monday, Wednesday and Friday. Play the guitar eight hours a day seven days a week. Sleep with your guitar. Name it. I named mine Liberty. Write a song to your guitar telling it how much you love it and take your guitar with you everywhere you go. She will be honest and faithful. Take her to New York City's Battery Park. Open the case and people will throw money in while you play with her. Go to the Statue of Liberty with her and ask someone to take a picture of you and her. Fly to California with her and play her on the pier near Santa Monica. Open her case and people will throw money. Take her to the beach. Take a picture with her on the beach. Go to the school where your sister teaches in California and play songs for the kids. Give guitar lessons.

13. **STOP PAYING YOUR BILLS** – you running low on money? Stop paying your bills. Don't even open your mail. Just throw it in a pile. If you open them you'll just feel bad that you don't have the money to pay them. So don't bother looking. Just throw them in a big pile of mail you are not opening. It starts to feel fun after a while. Kind of like a joke. Like I'm going to pay that bill? "Right". You will start feeling a little numb or like you kept getting punched in the gut and it doesn't bother you. So what's the big deal? They can all go to hell. I really don't care if the assholes think they can get water out of a stone. Let's see them do it. I just don't feel like dealing with it. I don't need the stress of looking at mail and bills I can't afford to pay anyway!

14. **TAKE YOUR KIDS TO CANADA IN YOUR VW BUS** – If you don't have kids, borrow them, No VW BUS? BUY ONE. Drive your VW to Niagara Falls. Go for a ride on the Maid of the Mist. Go over to Canada to see it from that side. Visit the wax museum. Go to Wally World. Camp out in front of it. Eat peanut butter and marsh mellow fluff. Go to a matinee movie and stay for two more movies to get warm. Drive back toward Syracuse to visit the Thousand Islands Canada side. See things. Go up in the tower to see all the islands. Get back in the bus and drive to Bar Harbor, Maine. Take your VW Bus on a ferry over to Nova Scotia. Keep eating your peanut butter and marsh mellow fluff. Look at all the light houses.

15. **TURN OFF THE TV** – Try giving up TV for a week and do other things: Reading a book, try something new. It is really amazing how much time people spend in front of the TV. I am sure over the course of my life I have spent years. That makes me feel a little bit sick to think of it. Of all the things I could have done or learned. No sense in thinking about the past. Now I spend very, very little time there. Do you really want to be a couch potato. I think not. The funny thing I find about TV is we sit there watching people live. They're moving and doing things on TV. We think that would be cool and the whole time we are just sitting. When we could be living.

16. **SEE A THERAPIST ABOUT YOUR THERAPIST** - Don't feel bad about seeing another therapist, especially about your therapist. Sometimes you just need to talk to someone and get a second opinion. I felt much better about my second therapist. Although he insisted that I stop talking about my first therapist. I stopped talking about my first therapist. I got off the drugs. That really bothered me about the first therapist – I felt like she was a drug dealer and owned stock in the drug company. The second therapist suggested another way to deal with depression. I was really happy to try other things. My hair was falling out and I needed a bra. Who would think something as simple as exercise would make me feel better. I think talking was also a big help. I went to group therapy with people who also had gone through or were currently going through divorce. There were others who were going through this hell and fighting to be with their kids. I was not the only person on earth trying to cope with this.

THERAPIST

17.   **GET FIVE GALLON JELLY PAILS** – If you try a donut shop first, you might get a better deal sometimes they sell the empty pails they get filling or icing in. If not, you may have to go to Lowes or Home Depot. You're going to need these pails for water. This is where it gets a little tricky. Ask a friend or family member if you can get a few buckets of water from their garden hose. They will probably say yes. Well you may have to get the water all the time. I might get it a 5:30 am, before they wake up or maybe after they go to work or late at night. Try to schedule your water pickups when no one is home. If you ask enough people then you can rotate the pickups. You did not open the mail or pay the water bill, so you've got no water. You will learn to conserve it really quickly. After washing dishes or brushing your teeth save that water for the toilet. It makes you appreciate every drop of water. It something like camping out at home.

18. **OPEN YOUR MAIL** – Ok. It's time to climb that big mountain of mail on your kitchen table. It's calling your name. All those shut off notices, the credit card companies, the bank foreclosure notices (those are the scariest of all). I could not believe when I went to the bank they would not take my money. They said I needed the full amount. It was 90 days behind, so they wanted three months payments all at once or they were going to foreclose. There was no way my boys would be homeless, so I got to work. Remember where there's a will there is a way. If I could do it so could you. I had yard sales. Took odd jobs painting, hanging wall paper, cutting grass. Anything I could get and came up with the money to keep our house. That was a real challenge.

19. **GET A JOB AT DOMINO'S DELIVERING PIZZA** – Deliver more pizzas than anyone else has ever delivered in the history of pizza delivery. Do this by running every minute you are not driving your VW Bus, while you are delivering pizzas take as many as you can fit in your Bus. If you get back before the other drivers you will get to take out the next orders. If they ask you if you know where a street is always say yes. Get a city map and keep it in your VW. Always be very polite to the customers. I also made more tips this way than the other drivers. It does not matter that it is a lousy paying job, still give 100%. Every time you give 100% to what you are doing you will feel good about yourself. The question is what kind of person are you going to be?

20. **HAVE YOUR UTILITIES TURNED BACK ON** – It is amazing how much you'll appreciate running water and hot water, and electricity when you have lived without it for a while. To this day I really love taking a nice hot shower. It is so enjoyable, I smile just thinking about it. Not having electricity is really a nightmare. We lived with a cooler instead of a refrigerator when our power was turned off. No stove either. We had an electric stove so we couldn't cook. This will be a happy day for you to have the utilities turned back on. I know we felt like we were in the lap of luxury having running water again and not having to carry five gallon buckets of water to flush the toilet. You don't ever feel the same way about what most people think of as necessities. They feel more like luxuries and are very enjoyable.

21. **STOP AT THE STOP SIGN** – We see all kinds of signs every day. When you come to a stop sign, let this be a reminder to stop obsessing about the past – it's over. Stop thinking if I had only done this or if only I had done that. You will make yourself sick ruminating about how you wished things had turned out differently. Stop. Focus on the present and look to the future. Stop beating yourself up about the past. If you want to feel better and have joy and happiness, then you must stop yourself from thinking negatively. Stop feeling sorry for yourself. Stop your whining.

22. **GO AT GREEN LIGHTS** – Just like when you are in your car. You will start to feel better about yourself as time goes on. Don't stay in the same spot, go, move. Try new things. Go to new places. The more you go the better you'll feel. It's all about experience, experience life. All the things that are mentioned in this book will help you move on with your life. The next time you're driving in your car, or for that matter, every time you're in your car and come to a green light, think about this concept. This is a signal telling you it's time to go ahead. Move on with your life. The road ahead of you is bright and full of adventure and excitement. So have fun and enjoy your journey. You only have life once. So live life to the fullest. Advance to GO!

23. **GET YOUR OIL CHANGED** – Yes, get the oil changed in your car and when you do it will help protect your engine and help it last longer. I am amazed at how many people will take such good care of their car and yet not take care of their own body. Pretend your body is a car – a high performance race car. Would you put any old oil in it or low grade gasoline? I don't think so, so maybe it's time to stop putting soda and other things into your body that hurt it. Try drinking water instead, not tap water but filtered or spring water. Eat more vegetables. Eat fruit instead of candy for a snack. You must have heard the expression you are what you eat. Your body is the vehicle that carries your mind and heart around so take good care of you.

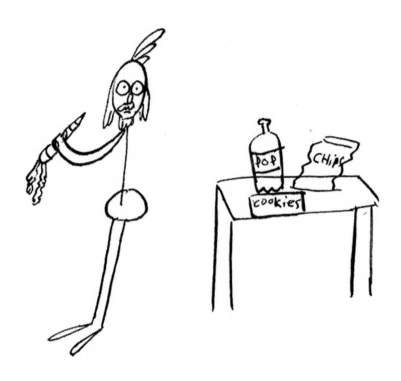

24. **START A BAND WITH YOUR KIDS** – called the Hobos. If you don't have kids, start a band with hobos. Have fun, make your own songs. Play at birthdays, picnics, camps, schools, anywhere you get a chance to play. If you've ever dreamt of being in a band, now is your chance, don't let anything stop you. There is always a way, if you are committed. Find people who love making music and start a garage band. I started with my kids in my living room. Jordan on key boards and guitar, Benjamin on drums and I was guitar and vocals. Who cares what you sound like, you will have fun. Let yourself go. Be creative. There is so much feeling and freedom in music. It is one of the things I enjoy most.

25. **THINK OF EVERYTHING AND EVERYONE FOR WHOM YOU'RE GRATEFUL** – I start with my family. I think of each one and how grateful I am for my two sons Benjamin and Jordan and what gifts they are and their health and talents. I remember the day they each were born and how grateful I was that they were healthy. Then I think of each family member and their family and how happy I am that they are healthy. Next friends and their families. After that I think of how grateful I am for my health and all of the opportunities I have been given that I was born in America. I got to go to school and all of the freedom I enjoy here. I think how thankful I am that I have another day to love. I think of family members and friends no longer living and how have gone to heaven. And I am so grateful that I had time with them on earth. Then I feel their spirit and joy. I think how grateful I am for food and water and shelter. This is something for which I am truly grateful.

26. **START A DOG WALKING BUSINESS** – Just think you can get paid to get exercise and hang out with man's best friend! I started a dog walking/pet sitting business and I can't believe people are paying me to do it. Dogs and cats, animals are so loving, so happy to see you. Pet sitters provide loving care and peace of mind. And busy people today, traveling for business or pleasure, are willing to pay commensurately for that important peace of mind. If you love pets, this is definitely a win-win. Using a pet sitter, the pet will remain at home in their own familiar environment and receive loving care they have been accustomed to. Helping prevent those problems so often associated with kennels and relocating a pet, such as infections, change of diet and change of temperament. And best of all you get to make another friend who is very loving and always happy to see you. Do you believe you get paid for being a friend? Win-win-win!

27. **CLEAN YOUR HOUSE** – If I have trouble getting started, I tell myself I will just clean for ten minutes. Once I get started it's not such a big deal. I am happy to see the place cleaned up and get organized. Sometimes I tell myself that when I get done I will have some ice-cream or a milkshake, which really motivates me. I also put on music I like or a motivational CD. I pick a room – like the kitchen, when I get done I move on to the next room. If you come across photos or gifts or other reminders of your Ex, take them down, put them in a box in a closet that you don't use. If the photos or gifts do not bother you or make you feel sad, then it's okay to leave them out. But don't try to kid yourself. I don't think you would be reading this book if you were not hurting. Sometimes it's a good idea to put out new things, maybe a photo of a place you want to go, Hawaii or Ireland etc.

28. **EXERCISE –** When you move you make your body feel better. Walking is a good start. There are many ways you can exercise. Ride a bike, play basketball, softball, golf, so swimming, jumping rope, tennis, climb a tree, dance, play hockey, play football, Frisbee, boxing, rock climbing, roller skating, Wi II sports games, hike, ping-pong, weightlifting, horseback riding, volleyball, laser tag, paintball, hula hooping, gymnastics, canoeing, tae kwon do, unicycling, trampoline, juggling, drumming, punching bag, skiing, bowling, treadmill, do jumping jacks, sit ups, pushups, badminton, have a water balloon fight, wash the windows, give a dog a bath, rake the yard, just to name a few. You can always come up with a way to exercise that is fun if you put your mind to it. So go exercise now and be sure you have fun while doing it.

29. **GO TO THE LIBRARY** - Just think about it. I know you are probably laughing, the library, why not just Google it? Yes you could sit in front of your computer and Google, but you will have a big butt (Ha Ha), if all you do every day is sit and Google. It's good to get out. Libraries are really cool. Some of the architecture is inspiring. It's like going back in time. If you had the chance to go back in time would you? The books are free, just sign up and get a library card and read as many books as you want. Who knows, there might be another person with a broken heart there. She or he might drop his or her book, you might bend over to pick it up and bump heads, look into his or her eyes. Is it love at first sight? Wait. Put your glasses back on. It's an eighty-five year old librarian. Well better luck next time. At least you got out of the house for a little while.

30. **GO TO THE CEMETERY** – The cemetery is a great place to go for a walk and do some thinking. All of these people walked the earth at one time. I wonder what their lives were like. Sometimes it's interesting to read some of their tombstones. Loving wife and mother 1920 – 1986. She was 66 when she died, I wonder what her life was like. That one has balloons on it with a stuffed animal 2002 -2004, "Our little angel, God wanted you in heaven". Just two years old, man is that heart breaking. Just think some day someone may be walking through the cemetery looking at your grave stone. What will it say? What are you going to do with the time you have left? How many lives will you touch? None of us knows how much time is left. Live life to the fullest. Don't sit around feeling sorry for yourself. Go out and make a difference. There are countless ways of making this world a better place, because you were here. Pick something you are passionate about. Help others. You want love? Well give love every day of your life.

31. **VOLUNTEER AT A NURSING HOME** – Bingo? Pick a day or night just one out of the week and volunteer for one hour. I pick a bingo night at a nursing home. Want to talk about funny? It's absolutely great. Here I was thinking I am going to do something nice. Well it's more like going to a comedy hour. The people are really funny. I almost feel like it's going into cartoon world when I get there. Their personalities are just like little kids. I guess when we get older we start to act younger. You will see how they try to win by changing bingo cards. There is one woman who will shout out the number every time I say it. She repeats it, then another woman who tells her to stop being a parakeet. They keep asking me to call their numbers, and when someone wins, well you would think they won the Lottery! They are so happy.

32. **TAKE A HOMELESS PERSON INTO YOUR HOME** – In hind
sight, if you do decide to do this be very careful.
Maybe you could volunteer at the shelter instead.
I rent houses out, so it really was not my home,
but a house I had empty. The thing about
homeless people is a lot of them are mentally ill.
I found this out the hard way. It was getting really
cold out and this homeless guy kept coming into
the Krispy Kreme Doughnut shop. I worked there
and really felt sorry for this guy. I would walk out
front and talk to him. One night I was leaving and
I saw him and asked if he would like to get
something to eat, so he hopped in my VW and we
were off. Now he really smelled but I didn't mind,
because so did I, but I smelled like a doughnut.
Well we got to the pizza place and people were
looking at us like we had three heads. We got the
pizza, but he had to have a Milky Way candy bar
on top or he wouldn't eat. "What" I thought, you're
homeless, hungry and won't eat without a Milky
Way. Okay so I went next door to a store and got
him a milky way. Then I asked if he had a place to
sleep and he said "no", so I asked if he wanted a
place. He stopped and thought for a minute, then
said "yes". When we got to the house he was
acting a little funny. Started telling me there were
too many germs. Well this guy hadn't bathed in a
month and he was worried about germs? I said
okay "what's the problem?" He said he couldn't
sleep on a bed without sheets. So we went to Wal-
Mart. The people at Wal-Mart aren't used to
greeting a doughnut man and his homeless friend,
so they angrily followed us around the store. We
got a cot and pillow. He took time picking that out,
it had to be just right, the right blanket. When we

got back to the house he was feeling a little bit better. I said good night and left him there. I drove away and thought to myself "what the hell am I thinking; I just left a crazy homeless guy in my house." Oh well, it will be okay. The next morning I stopped by the house to pick him up and offered to buy him a bus ticket to Florida. I dropped him off at the bus station and never saw him again. That was something else. You should probably help out at the homeless shelter and play it safe!

33. **HAVE A RUMMAGE SALE FUNDRAISER FOR THE NURSING HOME** - Pick a nursing home or charity you would like to help. Tell everyone there if they know anyone who has some old things they no longer want, would they donate them for the rummage sale? People are happy to drop off stuff after cleaning out their attic or basement or garage. Maybe they had a yard sale and had items left over. This is a fun way to raise money; you really don't know what you'll get, furniture, really funny looking lamps, old tools, books, clothes. Get a few people to help you price them. You will be amazed at how much money you can raise. Prepare yourself; you may have people haggling for the price. Be sure to tell them it's for a good cause. Then they might not be so cheap with their offer. After you are done call local shelters and churches. Ask if they would like the remaining items. They may have some use for them. The rest can go to the Salvation Army.

34. **BE A SKI BUM** – Get a season pass and go skiing every day, if you have kids get them ski passes also so you can take them with you. Pack a lunch and bring snacks, so that you can ski longer each day. This is a lot of fun, it starts to feel like you own the ski resort and your just being nice letting others ski at your place. I guess it is how a squatter feels. You spend enough time at a place and you start to feel like you own it. I always like to think how little it cost me for each ride on the lift up the mountain to ski down. I start to think that the more times I go down the mountain it costs less and less each time, and if I go down enough times, will they start to have to pay me? You'd think the more times you go up the more you'd have to pay, but not with a pass. Go skiing as much as you want. Just be prepared with a back pack of dry clothes and be sure to bring you own drinks and snacks.

35. **RIDE DIRT BIKES WITH YOUR KIDS** – If you really want to have fun, fun, fun, get a dirt bike and make sure you have a helmet on. They make a great bike for kids Suzuki JR50. That's the first dirt bike my boys got. It has a governor so they can't ride fast until they are ready. I would run alongside them as they learned how to ride, that's another reason to have a bike with a governor on it. Once they've learned you can ride your dirt bike alongside them. It is so much fun you will be happy you did it. It's like owning your own amusement park. There are so many things you will enjoy – just making donuts in the dirt is fun, going over jumps and on trails. If you'd rather have four wheels get quads. We ride them too or a go cart we have one of those as well.

36. **WATCH CARTOONS** – Cartoons are great. Remember when you were a kid and you watched cartoons. I loved Saturday Mornings because of cartoons. Sometimes I would watch them before school and when I got home after school. Bugsy Bunny, Popeye, Tom & Jerry. The Simpsons, the Family Guy still make me laugh. I am amazed how much fun I have and how amused I am when I watch them. Think of life like a cartoon and you are like a super hero, maybe Under Dog or another super hero. When you get up each morning put on your invisible super hero cape. Have some of that spinach like Popeye and start your day remembering that you are the super hero of this cartoon called life.

37. **TRY TO COOK** – Think of all kinds of food you like. Pick a few dishes and go to the store to get the ingredients. If you don't know how to make it go online or get a book or call your sister, brother, relative or friend and ask how they make food you really like. Give it a try, see if you can cook it up. I tried to make chili like my mom used to make. I asked her how she made it and got the stuff I needed. It did not taste as good as my mom's but I was happy I made it. There are all kinds of foods you can try. See if you can put a recipe of your own together, all different things you like. You just might come up with the best recipe of all time. Someone is going to be the best cook, why shouldn't it be you?

38. **TAKE A MARTIAL ARTS COURSE** – Karate anyone? Go to the YMCA or local college or phone a friend and find a martial arts course. If you don't like it, just try another. Sometimes it's just not the right fit, but give it a fair chance. You will learn a lot about focus and breathing. You will also meet people who have a lot of self discipline. That is a very good quality to have. They are there to help you learn. It is really nice to be in a class where you all have the same goals. You find people willing to help you learn moves and sometimes you are able to help someone in your class as well. It's just a good feeling to be on the same page as others. They want to improve too.

39. **DRIVE AT 10:00 PM TO THE BEACH IN YOUR VW BUS AND BORROW A SURF BOARD AND GO IN THE OCEAN AT 3:00 AM AND TRY TO TEACH YOURSELF TO SURF WHILE THINKING ABOUT THE MOVIE JAWS** – If you like scary movies you are going to love this. The water is so calm and if the moon is full it really scares the hell out of you. You can feel your heart beating out of your chest. When you finally decide to get out of the water you will feel a great sense of relief as you get back to the beach. Now look back at the ocean and think how crazy that was. You'll be grateful to be alive! Dry yourself off and carry the surfboard back to the VW Bus and go to sleep. When you wake up, go for a walk alone on the beach. There is something about walking along the water, watching the waves crashing down. Hear the seagulls, feel the wet sand and water run over your toes. Looking out at the horizon, it has a calming effect on the soul and spirit.

40. **CUT DOWN A CHRISTMAS TREE** – Be sure to wait until Christmas Eve and there is a blizzard. Then take your kids and a couple of axes and a video camera. Then drive to the Christmas tree farm and while you're driving video the snow coming down and your kids' faces. The look of terror while you almost crash the car while recording them. Then, when you reach the X-Mass tree farm because of the blizzard (breaking while filming) have your kids carry the axes while the wind and snow is blowing them around like rag dolls. Then, when you reach the trees take off your coat so your kids can lay on it while you each take whacks at the tree the axes. Video record it all. What a blast when you get the tree down! Drag it to the car and tie it to the roof. You will laugh as you drive away.

41. **LISTEN TO A MOTIVATIONAL TAPE/CD** – Tony Robbins is the best I have ever listened to and there have been a lot. You can learn and create the life you want. The sky's the limit. You can do this using no extra time, but while doing something else like driving your car or doing household chores. The most helpful thing I have ever done in the area of personal development started by just listening to tapes/cds. It will really make a difference in your life. If you go online or to the library or book store, read, listen, learn. Who says life's a bitch? I think they are wrong. Life is a beach and the fun has just begun.

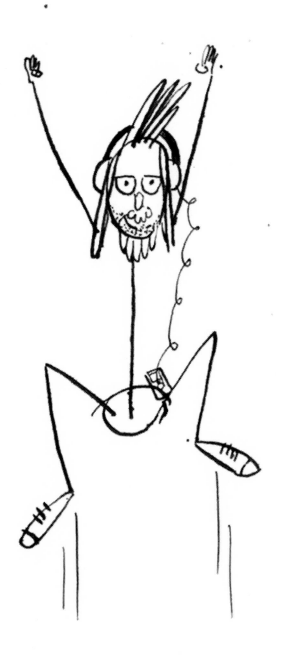

42.   **TAKE SINGING LESSONS** – Think of your favorite
songs and now you are a singer too, like Bob
Dylan, John Lennon, Tom Waits and Neil Young.
You are what you profess you are. You don't have
to have a pretty voice to sing. Let yourself go.
There have been many people who did not have
so-called ability or talent to sing that made a
great living from it. You are free. Sing any way
you'd like. Bullshit on anyone who does not like
your voice. You are singing for you, not them. It
really does make you feel better. Take your
favorite songs and sing them over and over. Make
up your own songs and sing them too.

43. **RUN IN A MARATHON** – Start your training slow, just go for a walk each day. If all you can do is a few blocks, that's fine. Walk a few blocks each day for a few weeks, then, double it each week. Before you know it you will be walking a mile. After that, out of your mile, walk or jog a few blocks each day. After a few weeks double it. When I was able to run one mile I decided to be in a marathon. So I told everyone I knew that I was going to run in a marathon. When they asked me if I had been training, I said "well I can run a mile, so in my mind I just have to run a mile 26.2 times". That did not seem so bad. At this time my brother Sean suggested I try running a little further, but it was up Delaware Street, a little steep, I thought I was going to die, but I made it there and back so it was three miles this time. Well I already told people I was going to run the marathon so I could not back down now. Just keep increasing your miles. My brother also gave me a book on training for the marathon. Well it worked and I did finish the Steamtown Marathon in Scranton, PA.

44. **BUY A HARLEY DAVIDSON** – Find someone who is always on the computer entering contests. They seem to win all kinds of things, cars, Harleys, Xboxes. They'll be happy to sell you the Harley they won at a great price. Use your tax return to buy it. You will be happy that you did. I am not sure how to explain it, but once you own a Harley you suddenly feel cool – something like Fonzie probably felt. You suddenly feel prouder, stronger, and happier now that you are the owner of a Harley. You are part of a culture. It's like being in a family that has got a lot of respect for each other.

45. **HAVE A GARAGE/YARD SALE** – Call your local newspaper, put an ad in saying Garage/Yard sale 7:00 am – 3:00 pm. Don't worry about getting it set up. I waited until Saturday Morning around 6:00 am to start. Well there were people in my yard at 6:00 am, and they will help you decide what to sell. It's amazing, they just keep coming. They will ask you "do you have any dishes?" "Well yes I do." Go into your house and look for whatever you don't want and bringing it out. They will haggle, but if you don't want it, sell it. They will ask if you have tools, clothes, furniture, etc. Just keep bring out all the stuff you no longer want and they will make an offer.

46. **BECOME A CLOWN** – Learn how to make animal balloons. Go to your local party supply store and buy a wig and some clown makeup. If you don't have enough money to buy the clown outfit, just make your own. There are books at the bookstore to teach you how to make animal balloons. The secret to learning is never giving up. If you would like to make some money, put out flyers or advertise in the newspaper "Clown for kids' parties". I started doing this for $14.99. I got so busy that I had to charge $65.00 to try to get less people to call. It is unbelievable how many people like to have parties and make their kids happy.

47. **KEEP BUYING HOUSES** - This is something that requires no money. Yes I said no money! Yes, I am one of those people who send away for the late night infomercial stuff on how to buy real estate with no money. In fact, I bought several courses on it and have gone to classes on how to do it. By the time I was 28 years old I had $750,000 in real estate and had bought some of it with no money down. So take my word for it, you can do it too. During my divorce, pretty much all of it was lost. That is when I bought my VW Bus and where this whole book started. But this is like riding a bike, once you learn you never forget. But you have to get back on the bike if you want to go for a ride.

48. **PAINT A HOUSE IN A WEEKEND WITH YOUR BROTHER DOOLEY**– Get up at 4:30 am and set up the ladder. The neighbors will love you for waking them up at 4:30 am on a Saturday Morning. After they yell at you, go and get breakfast with your brother and when you get back start painting. Look for any short cuts. I got a broom and a five gallon pail and tried that. Well it didn't work, but it was good for a laugh. Try a paint sprayer, maybe you will have more luck than I did, because that did not work for me either. We just ended up using brushes in order to finish in two days. We realized we had to paint in the dark. So use the head lights of your car or truck to see. No need to use toothpicks to keep your eyes open. I suggest you stop about 10:00 pm or, your neighbors will call the police. You can start at 5:00 on Sunday, just be very quiet, so the neighbors don't hear you. Don't let the rain, thunder or lightening stop you, just keep painting. We did and finished by 11:00 pm Sunday night.

49.   **LISTEN TO MUSIC** – If you pick the right music you will feel happy instantly. So why not be happy? I strongly suggest listening to the Beatles; man oh man, they make me happy. They remind me of riding around in my VW Bus with my High School sweet heart (yes, I had a VW Bus back then too). Now wait a minute that may be what you're trying to forget. Scratch that, just listen to whatever music you like! Everybody has their own favorites, so find out what is yours. Just keep listening to all kinds of music. There might be something you never heard before that will really make you feel happy.

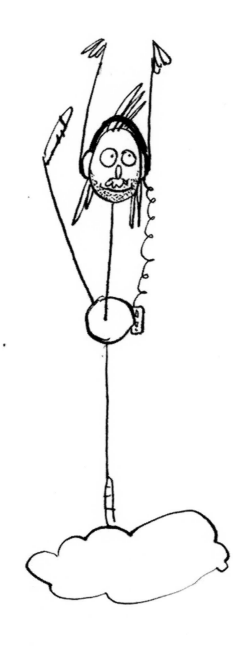

50. **GO OUT WITH A NYMPHO** – If you are missing sex, because you are no longer in a relationship, then go out with a nymphomaniac, which will take care of that problem. In fact, you won't have as much interest in sex after dating the nympho. It is quite embarrassing and uncontrollable; all they want to do is have sex. If you're in the car they want to have sex. If you're in a store, they want to have sex. If you in the park, they want to have sex. If you're at the movies, they want to have sex. If you're out to dinner, they want to have sex. If you're at a ball game, they want to have sex. If you're on top of a house fixing a roof, they want sex and that could be dangerous! If you're under a truck changing the oil, they want sex and that could be very messy. It's exhausting. Enough is enough already. Leave me alone. Unless you're a nympho too and then maybe you've found your soul mate.

51. **PLAY THE STOCK MARKET** – There are companies like investools.com for instance that give you a thirty day free trial. You get play money to play the market with to see if you are interested in opening an account. There are different companies like E*Trade or Ameritrade, which have low commissions and it's very easy to make your trades yourself without a stock broker. If you do decide to play the stock market use only money you are willing to lose. Don't, I repeat don't use money you can't afford to lose. It's important to educate yourself about the companies you're thinking about buying stock in. This is where a company like investools can help you learn how to do research about potential investments. I bought stock in Apple and was happy I did.

52. **GO TO IRELAND** – Yes, that's right, go to Ireland. Get a passport and set a date. If you'd like you can go to a travel agency. There is so much to see, the Cliffs of Moher, the Aran Islands, Inishmore, the largest of the three, off the west coast of Galway has a population of about 900. There is so much history there, castles from 1500 that are still standing. The air is so good to breathe. Each town has such tremendous history. I had it suggested to me that NOT EVERYONE CAN GO TO IRELAND. I think you can, but if not you can collect CANS and save that money for your trip. Every can collected helps the environment and gets you closer to Ireland. Keep cleaning and saving, Ireland awaits!

53. **GO TO HAWAII** – There is no reason why you should not go. Set the date. There are so many things to see and do. Staying home is nice, but travel is awesome. If you try to make excuses like, I have no money or I've got no time, well make time. I'm not telling you to get on a plane tomorrow and fly to Hawaii, but if you can on the other hand, do it, go tomorrow. If you need to set a date, see a travel agent or go online and do some research. This is really what life is about, living. There is nothing you can't do if you set your mind to it. The way I see it, all you really need is a plane ticket. When I went that was about it. Online a friend of mine found a person in Hawaii who rented a small efficiency in the back of their house. You really don't have to spend a fortune to travel.

54. **PICK UP A DEAD SQUIRREL OF THE ROAD, BURY IT AND HAVE A CEREMONY** – Just yesterday that little squirrel was probably having a ball running around gathering chestnuts and playing with his pals. His friends and family are probably really going to miss him. He might have brought home the best chestnuts in the family. His wife or squirrel girlfriend might be devastated. Now every time they look at the road they see him. It's not like they can take their little shovels, go out on the road, pick him up and bury him. Even if they tried, it's dangerous on that road. They might get killed by the big metal monsters too. So go do it. Get a shovel, pick him up and bury him in the backyard, then say a few words for him. Your kids will be happy you did and if you don't have kids, the squirrel's family will appreciate it!

55.   **JOIN GREEN PEACE** – When you say yes to Green Peace you will be happy you did. You too can be part of saving the planet. If we all do our part we can leave our children hope. I believe it can be turned around if just one person does the right thing and tells another who tells another who tells another and so on and so on. We can make a difference. There is a way to make this a better planet, their website is www.greenpeacefund.org. *"Greenpeace is the leading independent, campaigning organization that uses peaceful direct action and creative communication to expose global environmental problems and promote solutions that are essential to a green and peaceful future. Greenpeace's goal is to ensure the ability of the Earth to nurture life in all of its diversity."**

*Special thanks to Greenpeace for that quote and their terrific work!

56. **HAVE A FUNDRAISER FOR THE HUMANE SOCIETY OR SPCA** – These are great organization and worthwhile causes. We had a "Bark"-Bque and sold hotdogs for dogs. We sold bottled water, soda, had a raffle and called this event "Nature's Cure". We had people bring their dogs for a walk and as we walked through the park we picked up trash. This way we were cleaning up the park at the same time we were walking dogs. My Son Jordan's band played music in the park for entertainment. Everyone had a great time and we raised money for a good cause. When you take the time to help others or a good cause it has a way of making you have a positive attitude. This is something that you can't put a price on. Positive attitude can make your life whatever you want it to be. Do good things and good things will happen.

57. **BUY LOTTERY TICKETS AND GIVE THEM TO STRANGERS** – For just a few bucks you can put a smile on someone's face. Take five or six bucks and buy lottery tickets. As you go through the day give the tickets out. One to the checkout clerk at the grocery store, the person handling the carts, the person walking into the bank, the old woman walking into the post office. The person sitting on the park bench. This is an easy way to brighten up someone's day. Making someone smile is another way to spread joy to the world. There needs to be more people doing simple acts of kindness, so why not you? If you can make people smile and spread a little happiness, why not do it?

58. **GET A SECOND CELL PHONE** – You can do this on a family plan. If money is tight get a second job to the get the cell. Once you have the second cell, when you can't sleep at 2:00 or 3:00 am call yourself on the cell phone with your first cell phone. Now when you need support you can call yourself. When the second cell rings you must answer it as though your son or your best friend was calling and they need your help. It is very important that you stay in character. So Cell #1: "Man, this is killing me. I can't stop thinking about her." Cell #2 "It's okay, take a couple of deep breathes." Cell #1 "I'm trying, but it feels like there's an elephant sitting on my chest." Cell #2 "I know how you feel. Pretend you have a hand full of peanuts and throw them across the room, so the elephant will get off your chest." Cell #1 "Are you crazy?" Cell #2 "It works, just try it." Cell #1 "Okay the Elephant stepped off, but I still can't stop thinking about her.: Cell #2 "Okay close your eyes and inhale slowly, feel the air in your lungs. Just focus on your breathing. Hold, then exhale slowly. I will stay on the phone with you until you fall asleep."

59. **MAKE A ROAD MAP FOR YOUR LIFE** - If you go to any state, city or town you can get a road map for it. Well, maybe you go to MapQuest or have a GPS, but you still could probably find a map from the old days, say the 90s. How did people get from one place to another without a map? First you've got to know your destination. Then you can really start to make your road map. To get where you want to be takes planning. You know what they say about people who fail to plan, they should plan to fail. Not you though, you can do it. Look down at the floor where you are standing. Think about how that represents where you are in your life. You want to go somewhere. How are you going to get there? Are you going to fly? Not likely. Jump maybe, skip possibly, run, could be. What you need to do is take that first step. Therefore, to make a road map for your life pick your destination or destiny. If your name is Dorothy it may be a yellow brick road. Travel lightly and watch out for that witch and those damned flying monkeys!

60. **LOOK UP THE WORDS SYMPATHY, EMPATHY, COMPASSION, SERENITY, TRANQUILITY AND SELF-PITY IN THE DICTIONARY** - I can't tell you how much I love looking up words in the dictionary, and thinking "I like that serenity, I'm gonna get me some of that!" Just reading or saying the words serenity or tranquility make me feel better. Serene (a serene condition or expanse) as of sky, sea or light. Boy that sounds nice. How about self-pity? That does not sound too good, sounds like self-shitty. Definition: self-indulgent, dwelling on one's own sorrows or misfortunes. No thanks, I don't think I want any of that. If you think you're feeling a serene way, look it up in the dictionary. Then if you don't like what you read, look up a word expressing how you think you'd like to feel. Then say it over and over. Example: Joyous, Delight, Success, Good fortune, Well being. Start feeling better. Read about joyousness. How would your face look if you were joyous? Put that look on your face now. How would you move if you were joyous? Move that way now! Keep doing it. Be joyous!

61. **CHANGE OLD PATTERNS** – Think about the past 24 hours as if you were watching a movie. What kind of a person would you say you are? If you are happy, then that is great, good for you. But if not, then why? How did you start your day? When you get up every morning the first thing you should think of is: "Who am I grateful for in my life and what am I grateful for?" You can make these questions a morning ritual, just like brushing your teeth. Don't let random or negative thoughts start your day. Every minute of the day is an opportunity for you to be the kind of person you would admire. About half way through your day, maybe at lunch time, think again: "This is my life and I can make whatever I want of it. I have opportunity all around me and there is abundance everywhere."

62. **BUY A BICYCLE** - If you already have one, ride it. Yes, yes, yes, ride a bicycle. This is perfect. When you first learned how to ride a bike you probably fell off over and over, like everyone else learning to ride, but did you quit? I don't think so. You saw how much fun the other kids were having riding their bikes. No, really go get a bicycle if you don't have one. Once you learn you never forget. Just do it! Now while you are riding your bike look around you. Well, it's pretty cool isn't it. You can still do it. How does it feel? How do you feel, a little younger? You know what; it's also good for your health too. Fun and good for you, what more could you ask for? What's that, I didn't hear you? Someone to ride with? Well there's a bike club. People who get together to go mountain biking. Also bike races. If you just go to a bike trail and ride then who knows, there might be someone thinking the same thing you're thinking: "I wish I had someone to ride with."

63. **GO TO TIMES SQUARE ON NEW YEAR'S EVE** - I don't think there is anyone who hasn't turned on the TV New Year's Eve at least once and saw Times Square and thought that's crazy. Look at all of those people! When I went to Times Square on New Year's eve there was such excitement in the air. Everyone was happy, excited and cheering. It would be like being at the World Series or the Super Bowl and at the end both teams won and every fan in the stadium was cheering. It is powerful. These people are cheering to bring in the New Year and all the possibilities that can come with it. It's a fresh start, that's why they are cheering. The past is over and your whole life is ahead and the possibilities are unlimited. Everyone there feels like a winner. You're not a fan or a bystander. This is your life and the best is yet to come!

64. **GET A JOB OUT OF STATE AND SLEEP IN YOUR CAR** - Drive to Wilmington, DE and get a construction job working under the table for $8.00 per hour. To save money, sleep in your car. When you're working and you fall off the roof of a house watch how your boss runs over to make sure the nail gun is okay, while you are lying on the ground groaning in pain. This will make you appreciate – food, a bathroom, water, a bed, a warm place to sleep. It's amazing how good these things feel when you quit your out of state job and go back home. Apply to McDonalds, but don't be surprised when they don't hire you. Just go back to delivering pizzas for Dominos.

65. **GO TO AN ARCADE** – Go into a race car and go as fast as possible. Keep the pedal to the metal. Then, go to the motorcycle ride and go as fast as possible. That, along with other video games will help fill the time. Everybody has a favorite. If you think it's childish, you're right. What's wrong with that? Just try it. Pick up a video game or try the arcade, there really is something fun about race cars or motorcycles. I think it's because you can drive as fast as you want and when you crash you don't get hurt, you just start over. I know there is a little kid inside of you somewhere. So let it out and have some fun. Play games. Some people like SimCity or having an online farm, taking care of the animals. Others like playing war on first person shooters. Others play Wii bowling or tennis. Keep looking you will find something you enjoy playing. Just like when you were a kid. So be a kid again.

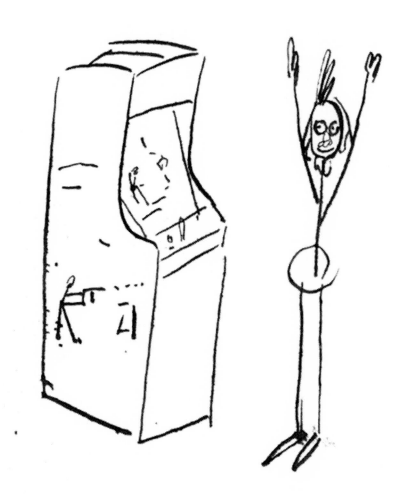

66. **Invite in Every Jehovah's Witness or Mormon on a Mission** – I am fascinated with these people. They really believe that they have found the road to paradise. They are usually very nice and pleasant. They seem to be happy and content. I just can't bring myself to thinking there is only one road to take to paradise. I'm sure they will get there, I'm happy for them. It's nice to see people who are happy with their lives. But the road I'm taking is a little different. I always enjoyed religion class in school. I like psychology and philosophy. I don't know. I guess I like to think about the meaning of life and how we got here. I personally feel there is a God (at least that's what I call him or her) or a force or power or whatever name people want to give love. You know the Beatles had a song: "All ya need is love" I think they were right. All you need is God = Love.

67. **TRY TO SELL EVERY TELEMARKETER SOMETHING EVERY TIME THEY CALL YOU** – When I get a call from a telemarketer, I repeat their name and try to sell them something. I just pick it out of thin air. I tell them I'm selling a time machine and I will give it to them for the amazing price of $9.99 a month; but that's not all. If they order now, by just giving me their name, social security number, date of birth, mother's maiden name, next door neighbor's name, cousin, friend and dog's names and dates of birth they will receive a set of invisible knives. In other words, I don't let them get a word in edgewise until they hang up or beg to get off the phone. It is quite funny, the more outrageous your story the more you will amuse yourself. So enjoy every time they call. The joke is on them!

68. **HAVE FAITH** – "How" you might ask. Okay, don't have faith. Well, wait a minute, I told you to have faith, then, I said: "okay, don't have faith." What's it going to be? Well that's up to you! Would you like to have a glass of water or dirt? Would you like to succeed? Or maybe you would prefer to fail? Would you like to be happy or is sadness more your style? You see the choice is yours. If you want it, there it is. What does Webster's have to say about it? "Trust, allegiance to duty, loyalty, fidelity, belief, strong conviction." Yeah, I think I will have me some of that faith. It sounds pretty good. Now what are your choices again? What does Webster's say about faithless? "False, disloyal, traitorous, treacherous, perfidious." No thanks, I don't think I would like any of that. Choose for yourself.

69. **GET CONFIDENCE** - This is very important. You can have it, if you're willing to get it. Think about the very first thing you remember. Maybe it is tying your shoe, or talking or walking. Okay, before you ever tied your shoe, did you have confidence that you could do it? Well then, I guess you just went for it. Did it work out perfectly your first try? Well, did you quit or keep on trying? How confident do you feel about riding a bike or driving a car? You see the secret formula for getting confidence is to go for it. Go right now and get whatever you lack confidence about. Go; don't stop until you get it. Repetition is the mother of skill. Stand tall. Move with confidence. Talk with confidence. Confidence will not let you down. Confidence keeps us moving until we succeed.

70. **SET GOALS** – Setting goals is a great way to make your life enjoyable. Remember when you were just a kid and you wanted to go somewhere, or do something, or be someone. Well there is absolutely nothing stopping you now. When you were a kid your parents would laugh if you said: "I am going to fly to Disney World tomorrow and spend a few days there ... then I think I will buy a Harley and drive it home." You can do, be, or go anywhere you want. If you set goals and take massive action, you will reach any goal that you set. If a 97 year old grandmother can lift a car off her great grand baby, anything is possible. Look all around you there are people who will not stop until they succeed. Never give up. Find a role model and keep moving forward toward your goals.

71. **REMEMBER THIS IS HAPPENING 4 YOU NOT 2 YOU** -
Sometimes when something happens in life we
think "Why? Why is this happening to me?" I've
got a newsflash for you. It is not happening to
you, it is happening for you. In the moment it
may be hard or even impossible to see. But as
time goes on, it will become clearer to you. One
of the biggest events that happened in my life
was my divorce. I was devastated. It felt like my
life was over, or worse, I was still alive but living
in hell. Not only was I losing my wife, but it
looked like I was losing my boys too. I really had
to hold it together if I wanted a shot at getting
custody. Well I did and got joint custody, thank
God. This experience made me so grateful; I can't
begin to tell you. Every minute I got to spend
with my boys I was grateful. How many people
lose their loved ones in an auto accident, from
disease or some other way? This taught me how
precious time is with all of the people I have in
my life.

72. **REMEMBER, IT'S ALWAYS DARKEST BEFORE THE DAWN** – Now is not the time to quit. You may feel there is no hope for your future, but I know where you are and I have been there too. I was literally at the end of my rope. I got a rope, threw it over the beam in the loft of my barn and put my head in a noose, just to see what it would feel like. As I stood on a chair, thinking, take that step and you will be happy. Something deep inside me said: "Don't Do it!" Although the pain was great, something told me to hold on. Life is worth living. I still felt unbearable pain, but I just knew there was another side of life I was not seeing. I took the noose off my neck and climbed down off the chair thinking, "What was that voice I heard telling me not to do that?" No. It couldn't be. Why the hell would God be talking to me? I have failed at everything in my life. I did not even have the balls to hang myself. As I walked to the house I felt a presence; a calm in the storm. Somehow there was peace in my soul. I don't know how, but I suddenly knew everything would be okay.

73. **REPROGRAM YOUR MIND** – Most people attain the greatest degree of success and happiness after some tragedy or traumatic event causing them to look deep into their souls. At this time they connect with their higher power, which I call God, and find their higher purpose, which places them in harmony with forces of the universe. 1) Connect with your higher power; 2) Visualize: see it happening, continue to visualize every day, this will connect you with your subconscious mind; 3) Move towards your goals, wishes and dreams; do what it takes to get you close to your vision; 4) Make adjustments where needed and never give up; 5) Share your gifts and success with the rest of the universe, success begets success, happiness begets happiness, love begets love.

74. **ALWAYS LOOK FORWARD** – When you're on the road of life it is always important to look forward. If you were driving your car down the street looking in the rearview mirror, it would not be long before you crashed. Well the same thing applies to the road of life. If you're always looking at the past, you're not going to get far before you crash. Look ahead of you and focus on where you want to go from here. Obsessing on the past does not help you move forward. Set a destination in your mind and forward march. You can get whatever you set your mind to, but only if you are moving forward. Just think of when you were a kid, if you had to stay in second grade and all of the other kids in your class were moving on to third grade, you might think, "Well it's not so bad, I know what to expect." Well, as time goes by, year after year, you wouldn't be so happy to be stuck in second grade. If you are not moving forward you will be stuck in second grade forever. Let me tell you from personal experience, two years were plenty for second grade. It's time to move forward!

75. **EAT AN ELEPHANT** – You may ask: "How?" Well, whatever the task is, no matter how daunting it may seem, just take the first step. Even if it's only a baby step. Just keep putting one foot in front of the other. To eat an elephant just take one bite at a time. Inch by inch it's a cinch; yard by yard, very hard. Break the task down into bite sized pieces. For example, if you wanted to build a skyscraper, you would first need to make a list of the people you need on your team: Architect, builder, lawyer (or someone to handle zoning permits, a real estate agent to find the land. Now you have a good start, by delegating you will be able to get the job done much quicker. Next, you plan with your architect how big, how much land you will need. Then you will work with you real estate agent to pick the proper land. Make sure that it is zoned properly and you can build this skyscraper on that land. After that call the lawyer to make sure it's okay to build there. Now, look for your builder. Now when they start to build they will start with this same process, making a list. One bite at a time.

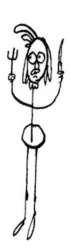

76. **WALK ON FIRE** – There's a Tony Robbins program called Unleash the Power Within. If you want to change your life dramatically and eliminate negativity this will do it. Things you were afraid to do will no longer hold you back. It turns fear into power – the fire walk experience does. You will not just be thinking about making it through another day after this experience. You can turn your dreams into reality. This is something you must do, if you want to overcome any fear. People from all walks of life, from 80 countries have been impacted by Tony Robbins knowledge on the psychology of leadership, negotiation, organizational turnaround, and peak performance. *He has been called upon by presidents, political leaders, world-class athletes, entertainers, teachers, parents and now maybe you*.* I can't say enough about his programs. You're just going to have to do it and change your life.

*Special thanks to Tony Robbins for all the help and inspiration!

77. **GO TO THE DOLLAR STORE AND BUY SUNGLASSES** – Every time you are feeling depressed, take them out of your pocket, stop what you are doing and put the sunglasses on. It doesn't matter if it's day or night. If you're driving a car pull over. Once you put your sunglasses on, close your eyes. These are magic glasses. Keep your eyes closed or you will go blind. These glasses have the ability to see the future. The future is so bright, you have to wear shades. Keep your eyes closed. Remember these glasses allow you to see into the future. Think about it. You must keep your eyes closed. Your future is so bright that you have to have your eyes closed and have sunglasses on or you'd be blinded. Look into your future with your sun glasses on and your eyes closed. Everything you ever dreamed of is in your future. You have so much to look forward to in the future.

78. **STOP WHAT YOU ARE DOING AND START TO SKIP** – Remember when you were a kid and you would skip. Well, start skipping. It doesn't matter where you are or who is around you. Maybe you will make someone laugh. That's a good thing. Skip, skip, skip, skip to the lou my darlin', skip to the lou my darlin'. I know it sounds like bullshit and completely ridiculous, but if you are not feeling good and you can't get your mind out of that rut, thinking about the past and your Ex, get up off your ass right now and start skipping. I mean it. Do you want to keep feeling like shit or would you rather be laughing your ass off at your crazy self? I know for a fact it works – I have done it! Remember, I am an authority on surviving a broken heart, if anyone knows how to make it through this, hell it's me!

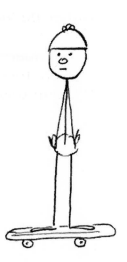

79. **LOOK IN THE MIRROR AND TELL YOURSELF: "I LOVE YOU."** – Think of all the qualities you'd like in your significant other, and become that type of person. Honest, loyal, kind, loving, generous, etc. You must become that person first and then you will attract that type of person. Remember, water seeks its own level. And just think you get to spend the rest of your life with that wonderful person, you. You really need to feel good about yourself first. If you are looking for someone else to make you feel complete, then you appear to be very needy and insecure and weak. You want to have someone to share your life with – that is great. But you don't want to come across as not being able to make it on your own.

80. **LOOK ON THE INTERNET OR GOOGLE NICK VUJICIC –** This is a man with no arms, no legs and he is happy. He is an inspiration. He focuses on what he enjoys in life and has a strong connection with his spirit and soul. Although he is limbless, I have seen him fly. His soul and spirit are so powerful there is nothing that can stop him from loving and giving. That is power. If you find yourself feeling sorry for yourself, this will help you to stop.

81. **JOIN A 24 HOUR GYM** – So if you can't sleep, you can go to the Gym. This is a great way to get yourself tired enough to sleep if you are having trouble in that area. I go about 3:30 am, spend an hour there, tread mill, weights, whatever you want. When you're there it's nice because you just about have the whole gym to yourself. It feels as though you own the place. There are people who have all kinds of work schedules, so they may pick a time that is also odd to go to the gym, but once you get yourself into a routine you will feel better. Even if this means going to the gym at odd hours. I have always had my sleep broken up because of work. That is why people take power naps. If you are able to sleep through the night, good for you. Then you can go to the gym before or after work. Also it's a great place to take a long hot shower. Enjoy it and save on your water bill too!

82. **BUY YOURSELF A VALENTINE'S GIFT** – I bought myself a new bicycle. Buy yourself something you would like. Something, if it were for your lover, you wouldn't think twice, but you normally wouldn't buy for yourself. Treat yourself as though you were someone with whom you are deeply in love. You are worth loving. Even if it means stepping out of your body and looking at you from the outside. You can do this by talking to yourself in the mirror. If this were your son or daughter, what would you say? I love your smile. I love your laughter. I love your honesty. I love your loyalty. I love your creative mind. I love your determination. I love your willingness to help others. I love your compassionate heart. I love you!

83. **BUY FLOWERS, BRING THEM TO A NURSING HOME, AND GIVE THEM TO SOMEWHAT WHO GETS NO VISITORS –** You have the power to bring love, joy and happiness into the world. So why not do it? There are people all around us who are lonely and sad, and just a small act of kindness (like flowers) puts love into the universe, which puts joy in people's hearts. To see an old woman's face light up it does something to your heart. If you put love, joy and happiness into the universe the universe will give it back to you. It's amazing what a smile will do. The next person you see, smile at, and see what happens. The person after that, say a kind word as well. Look for good in people and let them know you see it. Not enough people are focused on what's good in the universe.

84. **CHOOSE HAPPINESS** – Think of when you were a kid on Christmas Eve. Close your eyes, you will get a clear picture. Do you remember the excitement? Did you leave milk and cookies out for Santa? Did you have a hard time falling asleep? Listen and maybe you would hear him when he got to your house? Thinking about the presents you were going to get in the morning. You couldn't wait, and then somehow like magic it was morning and you could now go down stairs. Look! Santa was here. Then you rip off the wrapping paper and yes, you got what you asked for and you were happy. Did this memory make you happy? Every day is just like Christmas, when we choose to look for presents under the tree, open them up and be happy. When you wake up every morning look! You are alive, what a gift!

85.   **PULL YOURSELF UP BY YOUR OWN BOOT STRAPS** – The phrase was already in use in the 1800s as an example of an impossible task. By the 1920s this metaphor meant to better oneself by one's own efforts. The origin of this phrase is unknown. The year is now 2011, what is your meaning of this phrase? Mine is: anything you set your mind to, you can do. Nothing is impossible. You see, we are evolving. If you told a person in the 1800s we would fly to the moon or talk to people all around the world on a little mobile device or have all of the information available on the internet, that person would think these things impossible. Just as you couldn't pull yourself up by your own bootstraps. A lot has changed since the 1800s. So, are you thinking like someone from the 1800s or someone from 2011? If you conceive and believe you will achieve.

86. **READ THE BIBLE** – Did you ever wonder why the bible is in every hotel room? So many people misinterpret it. Maybe it's time to see what the heck is in there. Even if you just read one or two pages a day. Why not? So many people have read it, they quote it and say the answers are all there. Because I think just about everyone interprets it differently. As long as you don't start a war over it. Now wait a minute. It is time for a disclaimer: if any one reads the bible because I said so and goes out and starts a war or killing people, then that's not my fault. I did not write the bible. So you can't blame me for even what's in it, let alone someone's interpretation of it. I just thought you might be curious why so many people have read it throughout history and it is the most read book in the history of time. Amen.

87. **TAKE A CLASS ON MEDITATION/YOGA** – There was a race car driver named Joe Amato. He owned a chain of auto-parts stores – A&A Auto. Well, his brother Pete was not much like Joe. Pete traveled the world studying all kinds of religions and seeking spiritual enlightenment. He started teaching meditation/yoga classes. I was fortunate enough to go to some of these classes and they really gave me a feeling of peace and serenity. I really think if you get the right teacher, you too can have a feeling like this. It is really worth trying. Don't get discouraged if you have to go to a few different places to find one that works for you. It will be worth it.

88. **GO TO A CAR SHOW** – Start collecting old cars. You can find old cars in the newspaper, Paper Shop, or junk yard. I started with my 1978 VW Bus, it's actually a camper. There are car shows for people who just have VW's or Corvettes etc., but it's easiest to find a show for all cars. Back to my VW Bus. I bought it for $200 and took it to a car show with my boys. People love seeing this old VW. It needed paint and some work, but we still put it in the car show. We even got an award, when we took it to a car show in Canada (for the person who'd traveled the furthest to get to the show). Since then I bought a 1974 VW Beetle convertible and a 1971 VW Bug as well. These have all been in shows. There have been shows where I brought all three vehicles. It's a lot of fun fixing up old cars and looking at other peoples old cars and hearing stories about how they found them and fixed them. I guess you would say working on old cars is a labor of love.

89. **PLANT A TREE** – It always amazes me when I look at the little acorns on the ground in my backyard. The tree, in my yard, is so massive and it started out as this? Wow! When my boys Benjamin and Jordan were little, we planted two trees in the front yard, one apple tree for each of them. They were so dependent on us for water and protection from strong winds, they even needed a stick to hold them up at first. Well, they grew and grew and grew. You know what an apple tree looks like after fifteen years? I do. They are big and strong and give off delicious fruit. Just like my boys. Well it's time to plant another tree, but this time we are planting an acorn and that acorn is a thought. It is a thought that will grow and grow for years. We, you, me, all of us are going to be okay. Every day tell yourself, it's going to be okay. I am getting stronger and stronger, every day in every way I am getting stronger and stronger. Keep a positive mental attitude.

90. **FLY A KITE** – Did you ever fly a kite when you were a kid? If you did, you know how much fun it could be. If not, you should go out and buy a kite. In fact, buy three or four kites. If you don't live where there is enough wind, then drive to the beach. The reason I told you to buy three or four kites is because you can have even more fun if you have a friend go with you. Then you can have a kite fight. When I was a kid my brothers and I always had kite fights. What you do is you crash your kite into the other kites and whoever's kite is the last one to stay in the air wins.

91. **WATCH THE MOVIE THE WEDDING SINGER** – If you got dumped like I did, you will enjoy this movie. I have seen it several times and I still enjoy it. I sometimes think about all of the famous people who got dumped. Joe Di Maggio by Marilyn Monroe, Billy Joel by Christie Brinkley. This means we are in good company. All these famous people have something in common with us. They too have had their hearts broken. I know it sounds sick, but it makes me feel better to know that the pain of a broken heart is universal. No one is exempt. So just think, you're almost done with your turn and now you will be able to move on and live happily ever after. At least until you fall in love again and have it happen again, or maybe not. Next time may be forever!

92. **HELP A STRANGER SHOVEL SNOW OFF THEIR SIDEWALKS** – While I was walking from my parents' house after shoveling their walks. I saw and old woman struggling to shovel her walk. So I stopped and shoveled her walk. She kept offering me money, but I insisted: "No thanks I don't need the money, if you'd like, give the money to your favorite charity." As I was shoveling a neighbor asked me if I would help her and her daughter shovel, to get their cars out, if they paid me. I said: "Yes, I will help you, but I will not take money." After I got them out, they wanted to give me money. I said "No the deal was I would help you, but not for money." She looked at me puzzled. I said that it was my good deed and to pass it on. She then knew what I meant. Do something kind for someone else. On my way home I stopped and helped another person, the same deal. I often wonder if these kind deeds are still being passed on. This simple act made me feel very happy. Try it.

93. **BUY A WHOLE LOT OF FIREWORKS AND SET THEM OFF WHEN YOU'RE FEELING DOWN** – I got this idea from my childhood. Every 4th of July, all the kids in the neighborhood would get together at Harrington's kitchen table and make homemade fireworks. We would collect soda bottles and cash them in for money. Then we would go to Hudak's on Boulevard Avenue to buy: saltpeter, sugar, matches, cap gun caps, sparklers and whatever else was flammable. We had an assembly line going at the kitchen table. Two or three of us would be scrapping the gunpowder off the caps onto aluminum foil, the match box kids would cut the heads off the tops of matches (to insure a good flame). After that a little saltpeter and a wick from a candle stick. I don't remember exactly how we did it, but it worked. Then we'd go to the back yard and set them off. When I got older and had my boys, Benjamin and Jordan, I would just buy the fireworks. I had the money, so I would always buy way more than we could possibly set off in one night. So we'd always have a surplus. This is where the fun comes in. So if you're feeling down, set off fireworks, and this will lift your spirits. It always works for me.

94. **TRASH OR TREASURE** – What's it going to be? You might feel like you were a throw away, like a worthless piece of trash. Or maybe your Ex said something to you like, "I can do better than you." Or what my Ex said: "Eat shit and die." Are they right? Are you a piece of trash? Should I eat shit and die? Or maybe you're a treasure and they don't know it. Somewhere buried deep inside of you there is treasure. It's up to you to find it and share it with the rest of the world. I know this to be true: God don't make junk. It's the bottom of the ninth, bases loaded, the World Series on the line, full count and you're up to bat. This is your life and you are a champion. What happens to a lump of coal under pressure? It turns into a diamond. You are the underdog and everybody loves an underdog. Make a decision that you are going to be the best you can be and don't look back. Think of every area of your life and work on it like there's no tomorrow.

95.   **FIGHT FIRE** - When you wake up early, at 5:30am hungry for cereal get in your VW BUS to go to the grocery store. On your way home, when you see a house on fire, drive your VW BUS up on their front lawn, keep beeping and beeping your horn. When no one comes out of the house keep ringing the door bell, banging and banging on the door. Scream "get out, get out, your house is on fire." When no one comes out, climb up to the second floor and smash the bed room window and scream "get out, get out, your house is on fire!" When the family is out and the fire department gets there, get in your WV BUS, drive home and eat your cereal.

96. **GO TO THE DRIVING RANGE AND HIT SOME GOLF BALLS AS HARD AS YOU CAN** – If there's someone or something you're mad at visualize its face on the ball. You will be surprised at how much better you start to feel. Really, use every bit of strength you have when you hit that ball. Hit the ball and see that face. Now when you thought it could not get any better, start talking to the ball. Yes I said talk to the ball. My favorite thing to say is: "You bastard you stole my rice." But you can say whatever would make you feel better. I got this saying when my brother Dooley and I were young and watched martial arts movies. The action clips would be moving and the timing was always off on what the characters were saying. So we would pretend we were the Kung Fu guys and we would move our lips as we were fighting. We'd move our lips for about 45 seconds, then say: "You bastard, you stole my rice", as we kicked and karate chopped each other. It was a funny memory, but it works to take out you frustration if you hit hard enough.

97. **LET GO OF THE PAST** – Don't try to hang on to something that is gone. Stop living in the past. The good times you could be having now are being ruined by your thoughts of the past. You should not wish your Ex would somehow make you feel better. By doing those things, you are taking the power to be happy away from yourself. You're giving all the power of choice to your Ex. You're letting them control whether you are happy or not. Your Ex is not thinking about you now. He or She decided to end the relationship and has moved on with life. Your Ex has made a choice, now you must make yours. Your Ex doesn't control you. To get over it you must remember that your well-being is only in your hands, not your Ex's. You must decide that it's time to feel good again. You must start letting go of the past and start living in the present.

98. **GET OVER IT** – Only you can control your feelings and only you can make yourself feel better. Focus on the future. Accept that it's over. At first there is pain, nobody can feel it for you. You must make it through. Friends and family can love and support you, but you must go through it. Cry, yell, do what you need to. Keeping your feelings hidden will make it more painful later. Talk about it with someone. Just get it off your chest. You will feel that they don't understand, but because you are in pain, chances are, they do and are trying to make you feel better. Stop asking: "Why?" It seems impossible that this person you felt so close to no longer feels the same way about you. What matters is you must move on. Decide to let go of the past; stay away from emotional traps. There are many ways you can help yourself feel better and stronger, like spending time improving your skills and abilities. Exercising, taking a class, reading or learning to play a musical instrument!

99. **CHOOSE STRENGTH AND COURAGE –** The way I see it, you have two choices: weakness and cowardice or strength and courage. Just think about it for a moment. Weakness is feeble, frail, fragile and cowards die a thousand deaths. I don't know about you, but for me, I'd rather be tough, stout, sturdy and die only once. You really do have choices. Think about people in history who had strength and courage and I'm not just talking about physical. Think about Rosa Parks, Gandhi, Mother Theresa, Nelson Mandela and Martin Luther King. These people chose strength and courage. So I guess it's up to you. What's it gonna be? Are you going to choose to be a coward or choose to be courageous each day no matter what challenge you might have. I tried being a coward and it was not fun. Yes, I tried that feeble, frail, fragile bullshit; now I am going to be courageous and strong.

100. **DECIDE, COMMIT, AND RESOLVE** – *Decide* now. What's it going to be? What are your dreams? You want to make those dreams a reality? Put them down on paper; just do it. Do it now! Every morning look at that list of dreams. Feel yourself there; close your eyes and see it. *Commit*. If you are committed there is no dream you can't make into reality. Educate yourself. Find someone who has realized dreams and find out how they did it. *Resolve – (verb) to deal with successfully*. You need to take action. Dreams are goals with a deadline. Everything around us started out as a thought. Think about all of the people who dared to dream. The thoughts and dreams of the Wright Brothers got us to fly and Edison's dreams lit the way. We humans have been to the moon for crying out loud. If you can dream it, you can make it happen.

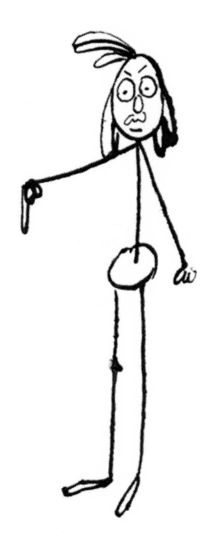

101. **BECOME A ZEN MASTER** – Study the Zen mind and spirit connection. Become one with whatever you are doing. Live in the moment. These are the keys, you have them. Every day you will thoroughly enjoy from the moment you wake up, 'till the time you go to bed. Feel the first breath you take as you awaken totally. Feel the air fill your lungs. Hold it there and exhale slowly. That my friend is the breath of life. You are alive! Feel totally at peace. When you're in the shower feel the water, be one with the water as it flows over your body. You are totally at peace. When you eat, just eat: taste, smell, enjoy. You are totally at peace. When you walk, just walk. You are at one with the earth; totally at peace. You are present in the moment. Your presence is the presence of the universe; you are one with the universe. Your presence is a gift, a gift to the universe and you are at one with the universe. You are totally at peace.

NAMASTE